Success God's Way...

A spiritual perspective on how to achieve success

IN EVERY AREA OF YOUR LIFE

ISBN: 978-0-9991830-1-4

Printed in the United States of America

Table of Contents

Foreword

"For I know the thoughts and plans that I have for you, says the Lord, thoughts and plans for welfare and peace and not for evil, to give you hope in your final outcome." Jeremiah. 29:11 (Amp. Version)

These words from the Lord, as penned by Jeremiah let us know that God is the Master Planner. He knows the plans that He has for every man. Therefore He expects for us to be wise and to carefully plan the steps that we take in decision making for our lives.

"The steps of a good man are ordered by the Lord..." *Psalms 37:23**

Anthony Luke *steps were definitely ordered by God** to help every reader to achieve this success by writing this book.

We need to be more aware of the importance of making plans in every aspect of our lives. His choice of Biblical accounts to illustrate the plans of God in the lives of His people helps to bring to life how God's plan(s) worked for them to achieve success God's way. Thus, reassuring the reader that through prayer, proper planning and by following God's instructions, we, too, can be successful. Our success, (doing it God's Way) will ultimately bring glory to God!

I envision this book as more of a manual that teaches one how to be successful in life by learning to look to God first for the plan and then following the plan that He gives. Anyone who reads this book and applies the lessons therein will benefit bountifully, reap the harvest of His riches, and soar because of seeking to be successful God's Way!
Apostle Patricia R. Gaston

Faith and Deliverance Ministries
Locust Grove, GA

What Readers say...

"This book is one of the best books I have ever read because it speaks to the heart of my attempts at success in own my life...It provided for me a precise method of planning in order to become successful. I recommend that you read this book as soon as you possibly can. There is great descriptive detail and the wording is fantastic. The writing is so good that I can see every part of the story like it is a movie inside my mind as I'm planning my success." The biblical story from which this plan for success derives is an awesome story which everyone should read.

Pastors Mac and Katrina Broughton
Turning Pointe Ministries, Inc.

What an awesome book! The book begins by outlining the steps to succeeding God's way. Each chapter of the book expounds of each of the respective steps. This is a user-friendly must read book for the body of Christ. It motivates you to shake off procrastination and begin walking in success according to God's plan. I love the book. It is superb in every way.

Elder Lester Paul Collins And Pastor Barbara Collins
Serenity In The Name of Christ Christian Center
1942 Conyers, GA 30012

Introduction

Throughout our lives, many situations and circumstances become the driving force behind our thinking, our decision making and ultimately our level of success.

These situations and circumstances can be of a positive or negative nature. **Usually, when negative thinking becomes the driving influence behind our actions, success is limited or halted.**

These *negative thoughts* determine the impact of our will or desire to strive for greater accomplishments. Selfishness, greed and immorality are only a few of the negative thought mechanisms that can *wreck our plans*, opportunities and *limit our degree of success*. On the other hand, unselfishness, good moral standards and caring for and supporting others can be the **cornerstone for achieving success on any level**.

Throughout our lives, we determine how and what thoughts will be allowed to mold and shape our decisions which will ultimately lead to success or failure.

So, how do we keep from negative thoughts or influences? How can these thoughts or influences be channeled or changed into positive ones which will change the course of success in our lives?

The following formula, which will be discussed in detail in the preceding chapters, is created by God. This formula has worked in my life and will work in the life of anyone willing to believe God and work the formula. We as individuals (especially Christians) tend *not* to inquire of God about our lives or our endeavors. We think *we have all the answers*. Nothing could be farther from the truth.

I'm not saying success can't be enjoyed without God, but when success is without Him, it's temporary. *(Matt. 6:19-22 NKLV).*

This formula for success includes these *ten steps*:

1. <u>Seek</u> God's guidance first (8:1)
SEEK - a: to go on a relentless search of: look for **b**: to try to discover
("And the Lord said unto Joshua, "Fear not, neither be thou dismayed: take all the people of war with thee, and arise, go up to Ai; see, I have given into thy hand the king of Ai, and his people, and this city, and his land.")

2. Have a <u>plan</u> (8:2)
PLAN - a method devised for making or doing something or achieving an end. *("And thou shalt do to Ai and her king as thou didst unto Jericho and her king: only the spoil thereof, and the cattle thereof, shall ye take for a prey unto yourselves; lay thee an ambush for the city behind it. ')*

3. <u>Know</u> the plan (8:2)
KNOW - a (1): to perceive directly: have direct cognition of (2): to have understanding of <importance of *knowing* oneself> (3): to recognize the nature of: <u>DISCERN</u> **b** (1): to recognize as being the same as something previously known (2): to be acquainted or familiar with (3): to have experience of **2 a**: to be aware of the truth or factuality of: be convinced or certain of **b**: to have a practical understanding of **(Re- read Joshua 8:2)**

4. Explain the plan to everyone involved (communicate) (8:4)
COMMUNICATE - a: to convey knowledge of or information about: make known <*communicate* a story> **b**: to reveal by clear signs
**(And he commanded them, saying, *Behold, ye shall lie in wait against the city, even behind the city; go not very far from the city, but be ye all ready.')*

6

5. <u>Know</u> and understand your <u>role</u> in the plan (8:5)
ROLE - a function or part performed especially in a particular operation or process
(" *And I, and all the people that are with me, will approach unto the city: and it shall come to pass, when they come out against us, as at the first, that we will flee before them...")*

6. <u>Review</u> the plan (8:7, 8)
REVIEW - renewed study of material previously studied (2): an exercise facilitating such study
("Then ye shall rise up from the ambush, and seize upon the city: for the Lord your God will deliver it into your hand. And it shall be, when ye have taken the city, that ye shall set the city on fire: according to the commandment of the Lord shall ye do. See, I have commanded you.

7. <u>Implement</u> the plan (8:9-23)
IMPLEMENT - to give practical effect to and ensure of actual fulfillment by concrete measures
(Joshua therefore sent them forth; and they went to lie in ambush, and abode between Bethel and Ai, on the west side of Ai: but Joshua lodged that night among the people. And Joshua rose up early in the morning, and numbered the people, and went up, he and the elders of Israel, before the people to Ai." CONTINUE READING THROUGH VERSE 23)

8. <u>Follow</u> or <u>lead</u> by example (8:9, 10)
FOLLOW - to be or act in accordance with <*follow* directions> b: to accept as authority: <u>OBEY</u>

LEAD - to guide on a way especially by going in advance b: to direct on a course or in a direction. OBEY
("Joshua sent them forth" {follow by example}... *"but Joshua lodged that night among the people. And Joshua roe up early in the morning, and numbered the people, and went up, he and the elders of Israel, before the people to Ai."* {lead by example}
9. <u>Remain focused</u> (8:18) REMAIN FOCUSED - REMAIN - to continue unchanged;

FOCUSED - concentrated in attention and/or effort.
("And the Lord said unto Joshua, Stretch out the spear that is in thy hand toward Ai; for I will give it into thine hand. And Joshua stretched out the spear that he had in his hand toward the city"

10. <u>Give thanks unto God</u> (8:31)
("As Moses the servant of the Lord commanded the children of Israel, as it is written in the book of the law of Moses, an altar of whole stones, over which no man hath lift up any iron: and they offered thereon burnt offerings unto the Lord, and sacrificed peace offerings.")

These steps are undoubtedly the key to success and have been proven to be foundation for which all believers and individuals alike have embraced for many centuries.

As a poor boy growing up on a farm in South Georgia I did not have many of the amenities of middle and upper class kids. I knew that there had to be more to life then what I experienced growing up.

The hunger inside led me to complete my high school education and go on to college and earn a Bachelors of Business Administration Degree. I worked on the assembly line at General motors for 26 years. I had several part time small business ventures that were successful, but there was something still missing.

I searched for fulfillment in many things only to remain empty. I turned to drugs, alcohol and promiscuity to find this fulfillment and while these things seemed fulfilling temporarily, there was still something missing.

Even after giving my life to Christ and becoming an active church member the emptiness remained. I realized that I was still trying to find success my way; this did not work. One night while reading my Bible, God began to speak to me and directed me to the passages of Scripture in *Joshua chapter 8. (KJV)*

After reading the passages several times I received the revelation that God had been trying to show me and my life was changed forever.

Learning to trust God and do things His way and according to His will is a growing process and requires patience and time. Once you understand His will for you, it makes finding success easier because you live for His will and not your own.
Each of the following chapters will explain these steps in detail and help to **strengthen** your **faith** and **trust** that **God's way is the best way**.
As you read and understand this formula, may the peace of God and His grace take you to places never even imagined.

MAY PEACE, LOVE AND THE SPIRIT OF GOD BE UNTO YOU ALWAYS!

Anthony Luke, Sr.

Chapter 1

Seek God's Guidance First

The Holy Scriptures teach us that **God** is the **creator of all things** and that all things belong to Him. Therefore, when we have a desire for a certain undertaking or have a vision, our first action should be to *communicate* with God.

We must do this for two reasons:
First, to make sure that our will is His will for us.
Second, we need His divine guidance and wisdom.

We are most vulnerable for attacks and setbacks after a great victory. An example of this is shown in the book of *Joshua chapter 9 verses 14 and 15*. Joshua made a covenant with the Gibeonites before discussing the matter with God and was tricked into believing that these men were travelers from afar off when they were Israel's neighbors and enemies.

Success depends greatly upon our faith in God's divine leadership and guidance. When He is left out of the equation failure awaits us because of all the unseen and unknowns that we will face from day to day. God helps us to achieve success in **our** season according to **His** timing. We can see evidence of this *truth* in *Isaiah chapter 28 verses 25 through 29* as God uses the parable of the farmer planting and cultivating his crops in season and making reference to Him as a wonderful counselor and guide.

Jesus, during His ministry often referred to God, the Father, as the one who directed Him, and for whom He spoke and gave commandments.

Seeking God's guidance insures that everything stays on course and that all tasks are completed and fulfilled as designed. *With God*, we avoid unnecessary setbacks and delays. His guidance means being thorough in planning and decision making.

We are all God's children. When we *listen* to Him and *follow* His directions any chances for error are greatly diminished in the same way as with which a natural father leads and guides his children.

Children who find that they are in trouble almost always turn to their parents to bail them out. For those who have a personal relationship with *Christ*, truly *wisdom* and *knowledge* from on High will be with them. *God* will supply all that is needed.

God instructed Joshua as to what to do and how he was to do it. God, in the same way will give us good instruction and leadership in developing our plans. We must depend totally on God, for He is our Father.

Nehemiah desired to rebuild the temple wall that had been earlier destroyed by the Babylonians when the Israelites were taken into bondage. He prayed to God for approval of his idea.

Chapter 2

Have a Plan

After seeking God's guidance and counsel, the next and most crucial step to success is planning.

Many times proper planning is diminished because we think that as long as the idea is kept fresh in our minds, that we will be able to figure out the next step.

There are numerous things that can derail or sidetrack our thoughts; therefore it becomes utterly important to **write down everything**. When you think it, write it down! God instructed the prophet Habakkuk to write down His vision, for it would not fully materialize until some point in the future.

An effective but simple plan is a VISION BOARD. To create a vision board you need a poster board, some old magazines and some scissors. You simply cut out pictures of things that attain to your goal (ex. Cars, houses, school, etc) and paste them onto the poster board. The vision board provides a daily visual reminder of your goals and accomplishments.

Proper *plans* that are *written* down will help to keep everything in order. Since every part of a vision or undertaking won't materialize at the same time, but in phases, *proper documentation* will keep each phase on the correct timeline.

Planning requires that a considerable amount of time be given to *research*. Once the vision or idea is evident in our minds; research, fact finding and any supportive information becomes crucial to the development of that vision or idea.

Research may start with reading articles books or other information that is specific to your goal. Then you use this research in formulating your plan.

In bringing our ideas or visions to full manifestation, our plans must include these three components:

1. Proper written documentation:
   This documentation may include reports, evaluations, appraisals, costs or other factual data.
2. A blueprint:
   The blueprint is a visual layout of the vision and what it will eventually come to be.
3. Financial Summary:
   This summary will outline all costs involved in bringing the vision or idea to reality.

Let's look at how these components work together by using the example of a homeowner that wants to build a new home.

The homeowner has a vision of how he wants the new home to look, its size and amenities. He writes down his vision. He then does research on property for its availability, local ordinances or anything that could deny acquisition and costs.

Next, he takes the idea for his new home to an architect to have a blueprint created in order that the vision can begin to take form.

From the blueprints he can now find a contractor and other building personnel needed to bring the vision to life.

Now that the homeowner has a clear understanding of all the costs that will be involved in the building of the new home he can create a budget and a financial summary of all costs.

The probability of success for this homeowner is very high because of all the initial and proper planning. He made his vision plain to everyone needed in order to see it completed.

There is much more that could be said about this step toward success. Proper planning through research and gathering of all necessary facts become the foundation for our visions and dreams. Visions and ideas are born in our minds, and then transferred to paper in order to lastly become a reality.

Proverbs chapter 20 verse 18 speaks of plans being developed with much thought.

"Plans succeed through good counsel; don't go to war without the advice of others." (Proverbs 20:18 NLT)

Get the picture? Just as one would not rush into war, great visions require proper and precise planning. As plans are developed, consistency and continued follow through will ultimately bring the desired level of success.

Joshua met with God and received the plan that would give him victory over Ai.

"And thou shalt do to Ai and her king as thou didst unto Jericho and her king: only the spoil thereof, and the cattle thereof, shall ye take for a prey unto yourselves; lay thee an ambush for the city behind it." (Joshua 8:2 KJV)

The plan is clear and Joshua is ready to move forward and take care of the mission at hand. Once we have established a plan, it's time to move on to the next step.

Another significant part of planning is the giving of information about a vision or idea.

Certain information should not be revealed before time. Nehemiah was careful not to reveal too much information too quickly. He only spoke to those on a need to know basis. Too much information revealed too quickly or to the wrong parties may delay or derail an idea completely.

So I came to Jerusalem and was there three days. Then I arose in the night, I and a few men with me; I told no one what my God had put in my heart to do at Jerusalem; nor was there any animal with me, except the one on which I rode. And the officials did not know where I had gone or what I had done; I had not yet told the Jews, the priests, the nobles, the officials, or the others who did the work. (Nehemiah 2:11, 12, 16 NKJV)

Chapter 3

Know the Plan

In this chapter, we will discuss the next step to becoming successful. One's level of success is highly dependent upon *knowing the plan* that is to be implemented.

To know means to perceive directly, or have a clear and concise understanding of even the most minute detail.

In the example of the house in prior chapter, the homeowner has a certain budget to complete the building project. Suppose he forget to include amounts for additional electrical outlets. While this may seem to be a minute detail, it can cause the builder to be over the budget and place completion of the project in jeopardy.

Joshua received the plan (for the defeat of Ai) from God, and he met with all his people of war and gave them the plan. *It is of vital importance for everyone that will be involved to know the plan.*

"And thou shalt do to Ai and her king as thou didst unto Jericho and her king: only the spoil thereof, and the cattle thereof, shall ye take for a prey unto yourselves; lay thee an ambush for the city behind it." (Joshua 8:2 KJV)

In Proverbs chapter 4, verse 7 the Bible teaches the importance of wisdom and understanding. It is very difficult to know something that you don't understand. That is why understanding is an important attribute to ones level of success.

"Wisdom is the principal thing; therefore get wisdom: and with all thy getting get understanding." (Proverbs 4:7 KJV)

Wisdom is the ability to think and act using **knowledge, experience, understanding, common sense,** and **insight. Understanding** means having the ability to understand something by having comprehension, insight or good judgment.

For example, in the previous chapter where building the house was mentioned, if the home owner did not take into consideration or understand the cost of light fixtures or window dressings and their effect on cost; while they may seem to be insignificant to the overall budget, this oversight could be very costly.

Regardless of the vision, all aspects of any plan must be thoroughly *understood and thought out from every angle.*
In Genesis Chapters 6 thru 8, the world had grown very sinful. God has pronounced His judgment on mankind. He instructs Noah to build an ark.

The ark is God's way of saving those who had not fallen into or repented of their sin. Noah preached for one hundred and twenty years that it was going to rain. No one listened. They saw Noah continually working and building the ark; the people mocked and laughed at him.

God's plan was in motion and Noah was implementing it. Because Noah *knew the plan* and every aspect of what he was to do, the building of the ark was done successfully and without flaw. <u>Noah did not waiver in his commitment to carry out God's plan</u>.

Commitment to knowing every aspect of a plan is crucial to that plan's success. Just like the homeowner, ones belief in his plan will bring commitment as it was with Noah in carrying out *God's plan*.

The plan was precise in every way: from the kind of wood, to the dimensions of height, width, and depth. The plan even revealed how the windows and doors were to be built.

In summary, there are many ideas and visions that have been brought to reality through good planning and understanding.

Ones knowledge of planning and planning techniques may vary widely, but should never be diminished or overlooked.

One must <u>commit</u> to his <u>vision or idea</u> in order to achieve the<u> desired level of success</u>.

Chapter 4

Explain or Communicate the Plan
To Everyone Involved

I easily identify with this step in achieving success because as a husband and father, I sometimes fail to communicate the plan to my family. It's easy to overlook the importance of having proper communication with family. Communicating with family in the ways that may affect or involve them in our vision or idea helps bring about success.

An example of properly communicating the plan with family is to get deep into the planning without sharing the idea with your spouse (or significant other). The communication must start from the onset with sharing the idea before the planning starts. This way, they will feel involved and be will willing to provide positive criticism and feedback.

In many instances, we need the participation of our families to help us get to a certain level of success regardless of how small their role may be.

The success of a vision or idea depends on proper communication and explanation of the plan to everyone that will be involved. Jesus spent three years with His disciples teaching and preparing them so that they would be ready at the appointed time to carry out His mission of spreading the Gospel to the world. The Disciples would ultimately have the responsibility of starting the Church.

Successful endeavors are never achieved alone, but require the help, support and expertise of others. Embracing the fact that 'we can't do it alone' and the willingness to seek proper assistance will insure a successful outcome.

Let's take a look at a football team or its organization for an example of the importance in communicating our plan to everyone involved.

In the organization, there is the management team and the players. The management team may consist of office personnel, marketing team, scouts and others with distinct responsibilities. Then, you have the players. While the management team does not take a snap of the ball, and the players don't have management responsibilities, they all make up the entire organization.
The goals of the organization are made known to both management and the players.

Likewise, Nehemiah knew that he needed help in order to carry out his mission of rebuilding the temple wall. He gathered his team together.

Then I said to them, "You see the distress that we are in, how Jerusalem lies waste, and its gates are burned with fire. Come and let us build the wall of Jerusalem, that we may no longer be a reproach." And I told them of the hand of my God which had been good upon me, and also of the king's words that he had spoken to me.
So they said, "Let us rise up and build." Then they set their hands to this good work. (Nehemiah 2:17, 18 NKJV)

Joshua spoke to the Israelites in the same manner concerning God's plan for the defeat of Ai.

("And thou shalt do to Ai and her king as thou didst unto Jericho and her king: only the spoil thereof, and the cattle thereof, shall ye take for a prey unto yourselves; lay thee an ambush for the city behind it. ')
("And he commanded them, saying, Behold, ye shall lie in wait against the city, even behind the city; go not very far from the city, but be ye all ready.") (Joshua 8:2, 4 KJV)

These examples of these great men of God serve to remind us of the important task of properly communicating with our constituents on every level and at the right time in order that our success may be achieved.

Have you told your family or friend about your vision? How will it affect them? Will they be expected to be involved and to what extent?

These are only a few of the many questions that need to be answered when an idea or vision is born within us, but are crucial to its success. Think about it, if you're needed to help bring the vision to full manifestation, then you need to know the full extent of the plan.

Many times we say, *'I know what I'm doing'* and that may be true, but we are part of the team. Therefore, it makes good sense for everyone to know the plan.

In summary, whether a homeowner, football organization or the mighty men of the Bible, the principle is the same. These men of the Bible show us the proper way to see our visions through by communicating with those we expect to be involved in our success.

Chapter 5

Know and Understand
Your Role in the Plan

This step is probably <u>the most misused or given the least amount of attention</u> in successful planning, yet it is the most *crucial*.

 No one achieves success alone whether in a household with husband and wife, or a global fortune 500 company. While one may be the visionary or the idealist, it takes the skill, expertise and support of many others to achieve a desired level of success.

On a football team, for example, winning the game against a formidable opponent means one must depend on the skill, expertise and support of players and coaches in different positions who work harmoniously together to achieve the victory.

In a fortune 500 company, many departments with specific tasks and responsibilities must work together with harmony in order to achieve the goals of the company.

In a household with husband and wife, (or with children also) all must work together toward a successful family life.

I still struggle at times with properly communicating with my wife on issues that are pertinent to our relationship.

I pray to God regularly to help me become a better communicator. I have to remain conscious of the things that are important to my wife and her abilities to make sound decisions about household matters and projects that may require her input and support.

This means making sure that she is involved from the onset; as part of the original vision, rather than halfway through and then needing her input or involvement to continue.

The department managers of a company must communicate with their subordinates so that everyone knows their role. The company president must make clear the roles of all board members and managers.

On the football team, everyone knows their position (role), so that when the huddle breaks each player goes to his position and performs the task at hand. This communication for understanding of individual and team roles are crucial for success because once the ball is snapped, it is time for action.

At that point, it's too late if I didn't know or I didn't understand what I am supposed to do, because the play is in motion.

That is why communication on every level that explains even the least role with the one expected to carry out the assignment is so crucial to successful planning. Communication is the bond that binds every person, department, or organization that will ultimately lead to successful planning.

In Joshua chapter 8 verses 4 through 8, Joshua spoke with his troops at night and gave them the plan for against Ai and made sure that everyone understood their role.

"Hide in ambush close behind the city and be ready for action. When our main army attacks, the men of Ai will come out to fight as they did before, and we will run away from them. We will let them chase us until they have all left the city. For they will say, The Israelites are running away from us as they did before. Then you will jump from your ambush and take possession of the city, for the Lord your God will give it to you. Set the city on fire, as the Lord has commanded. You have your orders." (Joshua 8:4-8 NLT)

For this battle to be successful, Joshua must carry out God's plan for victory down to the very smallest detail with everyone understanding their roles.

Likewise, Nehemiah had to make sure that everyone knew their respective assignments in rebuilding the temple wall as we see in Nehemiah chapter 3.

¹ Then Eliashib the high priest rose up with his brethren the priests and built the Sheep Gate; they consecrated it and hung its doors. They built as far as the Tower of the Hundred,[a]and consecrated it, then as far as the Tower of Hananel. ² Next to Eliashib[b] the men of Jericho built. And next to them Zaccur the son of Imri built.

³ Also the sons of Hassenaah built the Fish Gate; they laid its beams and hung its doors with its bolts and bars. ⁴ And next to them Meremoth the son of Urijah, the son of Koz,[c] made repairs. Next to them Meshullam the son of Berechiah, the son of Meshezabel, made repairs. Next to them Zadok the son of Baana made repairs. ⁵ Next to them the Tekoites made repairs; but their nobles did not put their shoulders[d] to the work of their Lord. ⁶ Moreover Jehoiada the son of Paseah and Meshullam the son of Besodeiah repaired the Old Gate; they laid its beams and hung its doors, with its bolts and bars. ⁷ And next to them Melatiah the Gibeonite, Jadon the Meronothite, the men of Gibeon and Mizpah, repaired the residence[e] of the governor of the region beyond the River. ⁸ Next to him Uzziel the son of Harhaiah, one of the goldsmiths, made repairs. Also next to him Hananiah, one[f] of the perfumers, made repairs; and they fortified Jerusalem as far as the Broad Wall. ⁹ And next to them Rephaiah the son of Hur, leader of half the district of Jerusalem, made repairs. ¹⁰ Next to them Jedaiah the son of Harumaph made repairs in front of his house. And next to him Hattush the son of Hashabniah made repairs. ¹¹ Malchijah the son of Harim and Hashub the son of Pahath-Moab repaired another section, as well as the Tower of the Ovens. ¹² And next to him was Shallum the son of Hallohesh, leader of half the district of Jerusalem; he and his daughters made repairs. ¹³ Hanun and the inhabitants of Zanoah repaired the Valley Gate. They built it, hung its doors with its bolts and bars, and repaired a thousand cubits of the wall as far as the Refuse Gate. ¹⁴ Malchijah the son of Rechab, leader of the district of Beth Haccerem, repaired the Refuse Gate; he built it and hung its doors with its bolts and bars. ¹⁵ Shallun the son of Col-Hozeh, leader of the district of Mizpah, repaired the Fountain Gate; he built it, covered it, hung its doors with its bolts and bars, and repaired the wall of the Pool of Shelah by the King's Garden, as far as the stairs that go down from the

City of David. ¹⁶ After him Nehemiah the son of Azbuk, leader of half the district of Beth Zur, made repairs as far as the place in front of the tombs[g] of David, to the man-made pool, and as far as the House of the Mighty.

¹⁷ After him the Levites, under Rehum the son of Bani, made repairs. Next to him Hashabiah, leader of half the district of Keilah, made repairs for his district. ¹⁸ After him their brethren, under Bavai[h] the son of Henadad, leader of the other half of the district of Keilah, made repairs. ¹⁹ And next to him Ezer the son of Jeshua, the leader of Mizpah, repaired another section in front of the Ascent to the Armory at the buttress. ²⁰ After him Baruch the son of Zabbai[i] carefully repaired the other section, from the buttress to the door of the house of Eliashib the high priest. ²¹ After him Meremoth the son of Urijah, the son of Koz,[j] repaired another section, from the door of the house of Eliashib to the end of the house of Eliashib.

²² And after him the priests, the men of the plain, made repairs. ²³ After him Benjamin and Hasshub made repairs opposite their house. After them Azariah the son of Maaseiah, the son of Ananiah, made repairs by his house. ²⁴ After him Binnui the son of Henadad repaired another section, from the house of Azariah to the buttress, even as far as the corner. ²⁵ Palal the son of Uzai made repairs opposite the buttress, and on the tower which projects from the king's upper house that was by the court of the prison. After him Pedaiah the son of Parosh made repairs.

²⁶ Moreover the Nethinim who dwelt in Ophel made repairs as far as the place in front of the Water Gate toward the east, and on the projecting tower. ²⁷ After them the Tekoites repaired another section, next to the great projecting tower, and as far as the wall of Ophel.

²⁸ Beyond the Horse Gate the priests made repairs, each in front of his own house. ²⁹ After them Zadok the son of Immer made repairs in front of his own house. After him Shemaiah the son of Shechaniah, the keeper of the East Gate, made repairs. ³⁰ After him Hananiah the son of Shelemiah, and Hanun, the sixth son of Zalaph, repaired another section. After him Meshullam the son of Berechiah made repairs in front of his dwelling. ³¹ After him Malchijah, one of the goldsmiths, made repairs as far as the house of the Nethinim and of the merchants, in front of the Miphkad[k]

Gate, and as far as the upper room at the corner. [32] *And between the upper room at the corner, as far as the Sheep Gate, the goldsmiths and the merchants made repairs. (Nehemiah 3NKJV)*

To plan through proper communication of specific roles and responsibilities, of all that will be involved, is not only wise but prudent to the expected level of success.

Chapter 6

Review the Plan

Since the success of an individual, group, or company's vision or idea depends on the expertise, time, and efforts of others as mentioned in the previous chapters; it is imperative that all aspects of the plan be reviewed constantly in order to insure a complete and thorough understanding of the part everyone will be expected to contribute.

Many times, emphasis is not is not put on the reviewing of data and pertinent information which is part of the overall plan. For example, with so much competition in the communication industry, knowing the price structure of several phone service providers could save time and money which potentially derail the budget of a project.

Reviews also serve as a catchall session for those who may have misunderstood or did not know their roles. At this point all uncertainties of roles can be cleared up. Anyone that needs clarity or more information should make it known to the appropriate parties or individuals. Also, if there are any changes or updates to the initial plan, this information can also be communicated to the appropriate individuals.

Things such as prices in materials or services can change the dynamics of a plan delaying its success.

In Joshua chapter 8 verses 7 and 8 KJV, *Joshua made clear the plan and the duties that everyone had been assigned.* All of the men we're on one accord in insuring that what had previously happened and lead to their earlier defeat by Ai would not happen again. Joshua was defeated in his previous battle with Ai because the Israelites had been disobedient to God In taking for themselves the spoils (captured goods) that were unauthorized. (Joshua 7:10-12 KJV).

"And thou shalt do to Ai and her king as thou didst unto Jericho and her king: only the spoil thereof, and the cattle thereof, shall ye take for a prey (keep) unto yourselves: lay thee an ambush for the city behind it. (Joshua 8:2 KJV)

Plan reviews should be done carefully and constructively to insure that all involved are ready to proceed toward the goal of success. Everyone should be allowed to participate during the review process in order that all questions or concerns may be addressed.

Chapter 7

Implement the Plan

 Now, after all involved parties have received all pertinent information and know all roles and details, it's time for implementation of the plan, it's time for action.

With precise decisions and accurate communication, the plan is put into motion. Just as the quarterback of a football team breaks huddle after receiving the play from the coach on the sidelines; and bring his team on the field for the next down, all of the strategic planning now begins to take form. All parties and systems are in place and the ball is snapped.

Successful implementation of a plan means winning the small battles or goals which will ultimately lead to the overall goal. As in football, each yard gained leads to a first down and every first down leads to an additional ten yards which brings the team closer to a score. On the other side of the ball, every defensive stop keeps the opponent from gaining yardage that would lead to a first down.

While different plans contain different strategies, they all contain the same ultimate goal. That goal is success. Whether it is success in winning a football game, overcoming family obstacles or learning a new job, planning is the key.

The plan for the football may contain these two strategies:
(1) offensive- to score points and move aggressively ahead,
(2) and, defensive- to stop or repel the forward progress of the opponent.

Let's look further at these strategies and their overall impact on the overall vision of winning for a football team. On offense, whenever the team has the ball the objective is to score points by moving methodically down the field picking up each first down and moving into the end zone for a score. On the defensive end, the team strategically plans to stop the forward progress of the opponent by not allowing them to pick up necessary yardage needed for each first down.

In the family, *Godly wisdom is the strategy used in the family plan to achieve a successful family life.* Key ingredients such as love, communication, caring and sharing are the cornerstones of offense in the family plan. These ingredients also serve as defensive weapons against hate, jealousy and immorality that can stop the success of the family plan.

On the job, the employee's plan for a successful career must include a strategy for communication with the employer in learning all job requirements and qualifications. These requirements and qualifications will serve as the employees offensive weapons for job security and defend against any misunderstandings or discrepancies and plots to undermine the success of the career plan.

Everyone is never going to be all in, or all out of agreement with a particular strategy or plan for success, however all can agree that some form of plan or strategy is necessary and vital to any vision or idea. Implementation of a plan or strategy must be timely and carefully devised in order to achieve a successful outcome.

Joshua knew clearly God's plan for victory over Ai. The offensive strategy was to lay an ambush for the city, lure its inhabitants out into the open and burn the city. With the city's inhabitants in the open and surrounded with no chance of escape, they we're destroyed. By burning the city and destroying all the inhabitants, this defensive strategy insured that there would be no retaliation.

And the ambush arose quickly out of their place, and they ran as soon as he had stretched out his hand: and they entered into the city, and took it, and hasted and set the city on fire.

And when the men of Ai looked behind them, they saw, and, behold, the smoke of the city ascended up to heaven, and they had no power to flee this way or that way: and the people that fled to the wilderness turned back upon the pursuers.

And when Joshua and all Israel saw that the ambush had taken the city, and that the smoke of the city ascended, then they turned again, and slew the men of Ai.

And the other issued out of the city against them; so they were in the midst of Israel, some on this side, and some on that side: and they smote them, so that they let none of them remain or escape. (Joshua 19-22KJV)

The plan was implemented to perfection and the victory was achieved. As mentioned earlier, the timing and carefully devised strategy of the plan insured success for Joshua and will insure success for each of us today in achieving our visions and goals.

Chapter 8

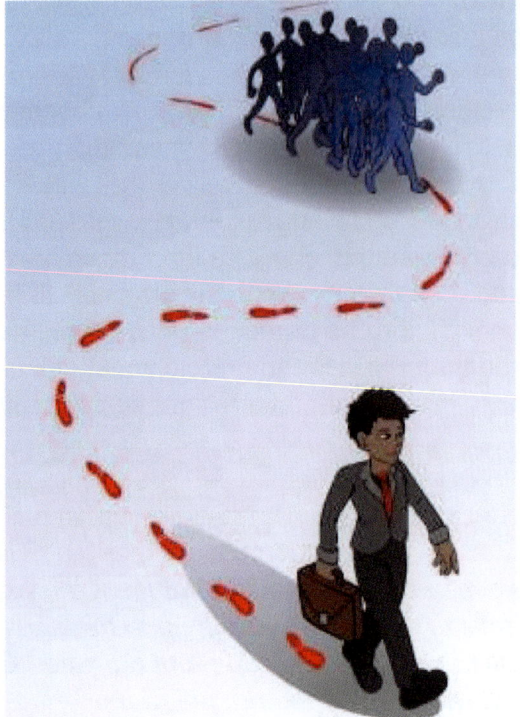

Follow or Lead by Example

Now that the plan for a successful vision or endeavor has been established and the roles of all participants are clearly defined and the plan is being implemented, individual efforts as explained earlier in Chapter 5 can be the difference between success or failure of the overall plan. *While each participant may understand their individual roles, these roles take on different characteristics.*
Let's look at the characteristics of two different roles:

1. The leader's role
2. The follower's role

First, the leader's role:

The leader's role is of utmost importance because most of the decisions, plans, and organizing are done at this level. *The leader must possess the characteristics of a visionary which can see the bigger picture.* The leader must be one who manages well and be fair and just. Success depends on the leader being able to make quick decisions and not be fearful.

Joshua was God's choice to lead Israel into the Promised Land after the death of Moses. *He has been one of Moses' most trustworthy servants.* Even though inexperienced, Joshua had the qualities that God knew would make him a great leader.

Now after the death of Moses the servant of the LORD it came to pass, that the LORD spake unto Joshua the son of Nun, Moses' minister, saying,

Moses my servant is dead; now therefore arise, go over this Jordan, thou, and all this people, unto the land which I do give to them, even to the children of Israel.

Every place that the sole of your foot shall tread upon, that have I given unto you, as I said unto Moses.

From the wilderness and this Lebanon even unto the great river, the river Euphrates, all the land of the Hittites, and unto the great sea toward the going down of the sun, shall be your coast.

There shall not any man be able to stand before thee all the days of thy life: as I was with Moses, so I will be with thee: I will not fail thee, nor forsake thee. (Joshua 1:1-5 KJV)

Being a great leader means knowing your mission and knowing those that will help to accomplish that mission. Joshua knew the people that had come out of Egypt with Moses, and he understood God's plan. He had learned a lot from his experience with Achan after the Jericho battle and after the loss to Ai.

Now God tells him that He will give him victory in battle against Ai a second time. So, he is poised to listen and be the leader that was God expected. Even as inexperienced as he was, Joshua possessed three basic principles needed for good leadership. They are:

1. Management of people and affairs

2. Communication

3. Fairness and equality

Joshua managed the affairs of God well because God was with him. We need God with us in all that we do. He managed the people that God had entrusted to him. Whatever has been entrusted into our care, we must manage it well. He was also good at communicating to the people each and every task that God had for them to do. As in the case with Achan, Joshua acted upon the Law which had been given to Moses from God. Every person knew the law. Moses had given the law of God to the people.

Second, the follower's role:

This role, however minute or seemingly unimportant, is just as essential to the successful outcome of a plan. *Followers are not out front and sometimes not seen at all.* For example, in a stage production there are lighting and sound personnel that have the responsibility of insuring those audio and visual effects which are crucial to the overall show are done without flaws. Yet these participants are not on stage and have no lines or script to recite. *They are not 'the stars of the show.'* However, the star knows that without these key people, the show would not go on.

In every plan, there will be those who work behind the scenes to keep the ball rolling. On the football team the quarterback is the field leader and receives the plays from the sidelines, but the players that follow him onto the field are just as important to the team's success or failure.

Joshua has great followers and he positioned them to carry out the instructions that we're given to him by God.

Joshua therefore sent them forth: and they went to lie in ambush, and abode between Bethel and Ai, on the west side of Ai: but Joshua lodged that night among the people. (Follow by example)

And Joshua rose up early in the morning, and numbered the people, and went up, he and the elders of Israel, before the people to Ai. (Joshua 8:9, 10 KJV) (Lead by example)

And the LORD said unto Joshua, Stretch out the spear that is in thy hand toward Ai; for I will give it into thine hand. And Joshua stretched out the spear that he had in his hand toward the city.

And the ambush arose quickly out of their place, and they ran as soon as he had stretched out his hand: and they entered into the city, and took it, and hasted and set the city on fire.

And when the men of Ai looked behind them, they saw, and, behold, the smoke of the city ascended up to heaven, and they had no power to flee this way or that way: and the people that fled to the wilderness turned back upon the pursuers.

And when Joshua and all Israel saw that the ambush had taken the city, and that the smoke of the city ascended, then they turned again, and slew the men of Ai.

And the other issued out of the city against them; so they were in the midst of Israel, some on this side, and some on that side: and they smote them, so that they let none of them remain or escape. (Joshua 8:18-22 KJV)   (Follow by example)

Good leaders possess these 3 characteristics:

    A. Humbleness – the people are as important as I am

    B. Good Communicators – explains the plan well

    C. Put the people's welfare before their own – insures that all the needs of the people are met

Good followers possess these four characteristics:

    A. Loyalty – believes in the mission and the leader

B. Humbleness – it's not my show

C. Respect – understand and accept the leader's position of authority

D. Accessible – Always there when needed

While there are other characteristics of good leaders and followers, you can see these characteristics in both Joshua and the men of war that was with him. Whether your role is that of a leader or one that will follow, know that it takes the effort of all for a plan to be successful. Joshua had been Moses' follower for many years before his time came. Ask yourself this question, am I the follower that I need to be that when the time comes I will be chosen for a lead role.

Now after the death of Moses the servant of the LORD it came to pass, that the LORD spake unto Joshua the son of Nun, Moses' minister, saying,

Moses my servant is dead; now therefore arise, go over this Jordan, thou, and all this people, unto the land which I do give to them, even to the children of Israel. (Joshua 1:1, 2 KJV)

Chapter 9

Remain Focused

There are many things that can be a distraction to us and cause us not to achieve the level of success desired. *The success of any plan requires complete focus and determination.* It is easy to become distracted when full realization or completion of one's plan is not achieved for quite some time or even for several years. Many writers and others such as builders start projects that do not fully materialize right away. Sometimes lots of money and resources are tied up into these projects and will not pay off until sometime in the future. Therefore, *remaining focused on the plan or mission is vitally important for its success.*

The player that does not concentrate on getting the play in the huddle or the fighter that is not in the proper place on the battle field because he did not receive the command or the investor that misses an investment opportunity because he did not get the right information due to being distracted are all examples of lost focus.

On the other hand, when the player gets the right play or the fighter is in position or the investor has the correct information; chances are more likely that the outcome will be successful because focus and concentration was not lost.

Focus and concentration requires uninterrupted effort in order for success to be realized. One must stay put, keep his eyes on the prize, stay tuned in, remain constant in work and be consistent until the end.

Joshua followed God's orders and remained focused n the mission. God told him to stretch out his spear toward Ai and he would give it to him.

And the LORD said unto Joshua, Stretch out the spear that is in thy hand toward Ai; for I will give it into thine hand. And Joshua stretched out the spear that he had in his hand toward the city. (Joshua 8:18 KJV)

Joshua made sure that all the men of war with him understood the mission as well as their role as mentioned in earlier chapters. *Jesus focused clearly on the mission He was sent to do. Even though He may have grown tired at times, He never lost focus of the mission.* He knew early on at the age of 12 the mission that was to be accomplished.

And it came to pass, that after three days they found him in the temple, sitting in the midst of the doctors, both hearing them, and asking them questions.

And all that heard him were astonished at his understanding and answers.

And when they saw him, they were amazed: and his mother said unto him, Son, why hast thou thus dealt with us? behold, thy father and I have sought thee sorrowing.

And he said unto them, How is it that ye sought me? wist ye not that I must be about my Father's business? (Luke 2:46-49 KJV)

Because Jesus was focused and fully involved, we today have access to God through Him. As Christians, we must remain focused on our divine mission to bring the Good News to all that will hear through the spread of the Gospel of Jesus which is the Word of God.

Thomas saith unto him, Lord, we know not whither thou goest; and how can we know the way?

Jesus saith unto him, I am the way, the truth, and the life: no man cometh unto the Father, but by me.

If ye had known me, ye should have known my Father also: and from henceforth ye know him, and have seen him. (John 14: 5-7 KJV)

And Jesus answered them, saying, The hour is come, that the Son of man should be glorified.

Verily, verily, I say unto you, Except a corn of wheat fall into the ground and die, it abideth alone: but if it die, it bringeth forth much fruit.

He that loveth his life shall lose it; and he that hateth his life in this world shall keep it unto life eternal.

If any man serve me, let him follow me; and where I am, there shall also my servant be: if any man serve me, him will my Father honour.

Now is my soul troubled; and what shall I say? Father, save me from this hour: but for this cause came I unto this hour. (John 12:23-27 KJV)

Chapter 10

Give Thanks unto God

It is easy after a successful endeavor to pat yourself on the back or receive many accolades but the truth is that without the grace, mercy and counsel of Almighty God, our success would be minimal at best. Therefore, it is of utmost importance to give just due to whom it is deserved. *God and only God alone deserve the credit for every ounce of success that we ever realize.*

Think about it, what is success without God? We remain empty, void and full of uncertainties, but many realize that after the buzz is gone and things are back to normal that there is still a void. *Many statements spoken after success is realized such as: 'I did my part' or 'I did what I was supposed to do' or 'I'm the MVP' or 'I won the championship' may bring moments of temporary gratification.* Because of this void that is left within us, we're off to the next challenge searching for that inner fulfillment.

The type of fulfillment experienced after success through God has the greatest reward and is life changing. *This reward is not realized from a trophy in the trophy case or a big bonus check*, but the realization of knowing without a doubt that God was pleased with your efforts and His rewards are eternal. The rewards of inner peace, joy and love are only realized after God has walked with us through our successes.
This is why He alone deserves all thanks and praises for our successes.

God also rewards our successes with name changes. Changes such as, *'Abram to Abraham'* or *'Jacob to Israel'* or *'Servant to Son'* or *'Failure to Success'* and so on are part of God's reward. When we are obedient to God's will for our lives, we may have been known as failures in the past but one successful endeavor through God changes everything forever.

Joshua and the children of Israel gave thanks to God for their successful victory by offering burnt and peace offerings unto Him.

Then Joshua built an altar unto the LORD God of Israel in mount Ebal, As Moses the servant of the LORD commanded the children of Israel, as it is written in the book of the law of Moses, an altar of whole stones, over which no man hath lift up any iron: and they offered thereon burnt offerings unto the LORD, and sacrificed peace offerings. (Joshua 8:30, 31 KJV)

Mordecai recorded the events of the Jews victory over their enemy and sent letters throughout all the provinces of King Ahasuerus reminding all to *celebrate annually on the fourteenth and fifteenth day* of the Jewish month of Adar (that is the twelfth month of the

Jewish calendar) which starts from the middle of February and runs through the middle of March.

And Mordecai wrote these things, and sent letters unto all the Jews that were in all the provinces of the king Ahasuerus, both nigh and far,

To stablish this among them, that they should keep the fourteenth day of the month Adar, and the fifteenth day of the same, yearly,

As the days wherein the Jews rested from their enemies, and the month which was turned unto them from sorrow to joy, and from mourning into a good day: that they should make them days of feasting and joy, and of sending portions one to another, and gifts to the poor. (Esther 9:20-22 KJV)

His rewards are eternal; therefore, His thanks from us for our successes must be from the heart where we all love and admonish Him eternally through His son Jesus Christ.

How do you celebrate your successes? Do you give God glory and praise for all that He has done? *An inward change in our hearts and minds will flow out with great joy and peace.* Because as believers; we understand that without God, true and eternal success that builds inner character, strength and power cannot be realized through physical accomplishments. While physical accomplishments will bring some gratification, it only lasts for a period of time and then we are looking for the next challenge.

Success in God brings everlasting joy and fulfillment that will last for eternity, supply our hearts and spirits with comfort while helping us to know that we have all we need in Christ. Therefore, our fulfillment is complete and we don't have to keep searching for the next challenge.

May the grace of God keep you and His blessings prosper you to success in every way. Give Him praise and glory for all things and enjoy success through Him in every way.

Acknowledgements

First and foremost, I want to thank God Almighty for His spirit that guided me through this project. I know that without His divine inspiration and grace, this project could not have been completed. Many days and nights, I asked God for the words to write and how He would have me present the information, because this is not my project but His. I am eternally grateful that He chose me to bring it to the world. I hope that you the reader will feel the love of God, made available through Christ as you apply these principles into your life.

To God be the glory always.

To my wife, Sandra

There we're many times when you wondered what I was doing spending so much time on the computer. I want to thank you for not giving up on me and believing in me. I know how much you love God and because of that love, you were able to hang in there with me. You are truly a gift from God to me and I love you with all my heart. I thank Him for you every day of my life.
I am proud to be your husband.

I Love you, Baby. You have and will always be my forever love. I pray that God will continue to be center of your joy as He is mine and that He will continue to Shower His blessings upon us.

With all my love,

Tony

To Apostle Pat Gaston

I thank you Apostle Gaston for your encouragement and inspiring me to continue this project. Over the last three years, your encouraging emails and conversations have been truly uplifting. I thank God for you also. You make sure that my grammar is correct and all my sentences are complete.

May God continue to smile upon you and family even more than before? May your latter days be greater than your former days!

God Bless,

Brother Luke

To Barbara Lucas

Your knowledge and expertise has meant everything to the completion of this book. From the depths of my heart, THANK YOU. I could not have completed this work without your knowledge and input. It's people like you that make a difference in the lives of others. May God eternally bless you in all that you do.

To John Thomas (Jay Tee)

Your input and expertise is invaluable. Words cannot express the thanks you're due for your creative influence and technical skills. Continue the great work you are doing for the Kingdom and may God be with you always!

Tony

To Renato Capasso

Your perfection is beyond measure. Thanks for the great images you created for me that illustrate each chapter. May God continue to bless you.

References

All scripture references, passages and verses used to illustrate and explain the before mentioned success steps are taken from the *King James, New Living Translation, Amplified, and New King James Version* of the Holy Bible.

About the Author

Being born to a single Mom who saw the need to let me go and be raised from the age of six by my Aunt (her older sister) and uncle because she struggled to make ends meet and to grow up not understanding why life was so hard made me wonder if God was punishing us. It took courage for Mom to say go with them and have a better life which did not turn out that way.

It was years later that I realized the deepness of that love to let go of someone as cherishing as a child and to somehow never forgive yourself for it until years later. Our path is not known, but we must never lose sight of the fact that God knows best.

It was through this early experience that God began to shape my thoughts and desires not only to improve myself but to inspire others as well. Even when I didn't know it was God, He was working things out behind the scenes for my good.

While I could tell you about my accomplishments and failures, I rather tell you that if you trust God with your life, you'll never lose it but gain it for time everlasting.

Anthony Luke, Sr

Printed in Dunstable, United Kingdom